I LOVE AFRICA

I LOVE AFRICA

CAROLE AYRES

XULON PRESS

Xulon Press
2301 Lucien Way #415
Maitland, FL 32751
407.339.4217
www.xulonpress.com

© 2018 by Carole Ayres

All rights reserved solely by the author. The author guarantees all contents are original and do not infringe upon the legal rights of any other person or work. No part of this book may be reproduced in any form without the permission of the author. The views expressed in this book are not necessarily those of the publisher.

Printed in the United States of America.

Photo credit for Map of Africa: Maphill.com.

ISBN-13: 9781545622872

Dear reader,

Come along my trip to Africa! You will find a felucca sailboat on the Nile River in Egypt, an old man reading a book with a magnifying glass at a souk (marketplace) in Morocco, and a 650-pound gorilla in Rwanda. That is only North Africa! Next, you will see the gigantic Victoria Falls in Zambia, Mr. and Mrs. Lion on the Serengeti Plain in Tanzania, and a three-foot-tall lemur on the island of Madagascar in the Indian Ocean. We travel to South Africa to see the Atlantic and Pacific Oceans meet at the Cape of Good Hope.

In Namibia, a fire dancer (called a poi spinner) dances in the dark and a seal jumps onto our boat at breakfast in Walvis Bay. In Mali, we watch Dogon dancers show us a tale of hunters. Our tour ends in Morocco, where we say farewell to all our new friends.

Carole Ayres

For Caroline, Charlie, Sadie, Carson, Campbell, Kade, and Keegan

Oh, Africa, what a mysterious ancient land!
With mountains, oceans, winding rivers, and desert sand,
Stunning valleys and sand dunes, seashores and boats.
Child, come with me to see these lands, so remote.

You will love Africa for so many amazing things.
The people, animals, and the wonder it brings.
Ride a camel in Egypt. Row a felucca on River Nile.
Climb onto an elephant in Zambia for a while.

Sit by the fire on the Serengeti Plain.
Listen for the animals, but be careful. They are not tame.
You should have seen the lions I watched one day.
Oh, my goodness, they were only ten yards away!

Look into this enchanting wild place,
Collect marvelous memories your mind will never erase.
Wild animals galore---Africa hosts so many!
To the continent of Africa, God gave plenty.

I hiked for a while in Rwanda one day,
To sit with a gorilla family as they snacked on hay.
In wild-eyed amazement, we watched them eat.
We sat strangely close to them; it was really a treat!

Once in a while the dad, Gahundi, peered at us,
To make sure we were not making a fuss.
We smiled thankfully, trying to understand,
What a gift it was to share this grand land.

You must see Victoria Falls in Zambia! It is glorious.
Zambezi River water crashed 355 feet,
to the pebble floor beneath us.
Under our umbrellas,
we peeked through mist to spot rainbows and clouds,
But we could not hear a human or bird,
because the booming falls were so loud.

They sounded like thunder. We felt very small.
As the tumbling water in front of us created a huge wall,
We yelled to each other, but we just could not hear.
So, we simply admired it, and grinned with good cheer.

In South Africa, a cable car took us for a bumpy ride,
To Table Mountain, where we saw oceans collide.
The Cape of Good Hope is located here, where,
The Indian and Atlantic Oceans into one another disappear.

Namibia was truly our must unusual day,
For hours in the desert, you can play.
Airplanes, four-wheelers, dinner in the desert at night,
Parachutes at sunset filled us with delight.

Fire dancers and drums. Dinner by candlelight.
Flames lit up the canyon walls; we could have danced all night.
Exhausted, and full of joy and wonder,
We rode back to our hotel and collapsed in slumber.

Up early the next day, we sped off on a boat,
To eat oysters for breakfast while wearing raincoats.
Oti the seal jumped aboard for a look and a bite.
Breakfast with a seal was a humorous sight.

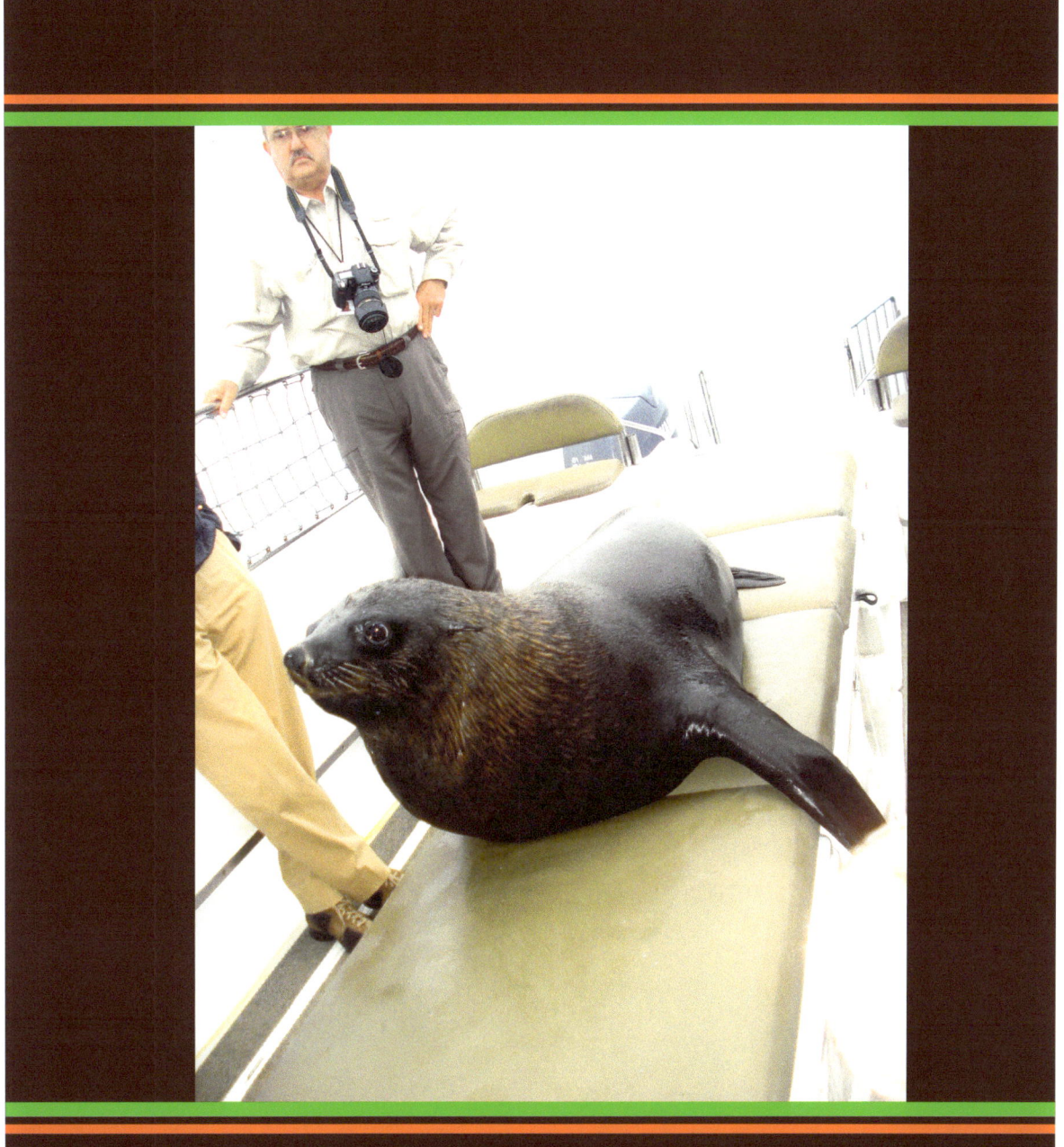

Off to Mali, we went the next day.
We watched dancers on stilts put on a play.
In a marketplace, we stopped to shop,
But on a pinasse on Niger River, we never did stop.

On our last stop we gathered to say goodbye.
Our fellow adventurers gave big, sad sighs.
Morocco smelled like spices; it is a lovely place.
Our final celebration held warmth and grace.

Thank you for reading with me, with love and care,
For beautiful Africa! I am so glad I could share.
Someday soon, I hope you can go,
To this glorious land and see its magnificent show.

ABOUT THE AUTHOR

Author Carole Ayres peeks through a door in Marrakech, Morocco

Carole Ayres grew up in Tennessee, and resides there with her husband Joe (pictured with the elephant) and their three sons, two daughters-in-law, and seven grandchildren. Carole is a retired teacher, but tutors English language learners. With her family, Carole enjoys spending time outdoors—from hiking the Great Smoky Mountains and boating Douglas Lake in Tennessee, to skiing Colorado slopes or exploring the beaches of Turks and Caicos. Carole is a world-traveler who loves sharing her passion for discovery with young people.

Look for other *I LOVE* books by Carole Ayres on Amazon.com.